SOCIAL SECURITY
The Story of Its Past and a Vision for Its Future

SOCIAL SECURITY
The Story of Its Past and a Vision for Its Future

Andrew G. Biggs

AEI Press

Publisher for the American Enterprise Institute
Washington, D.C.

Distributed by arrangement with the National Book Network
15200 NBN Way, Blue Ridge Summit, PA 17214
To order call toll free 1-800-462-6420 or 1-717-794-3800.

For all other inquiries please contact AEI Press, 1150 17th Street,
N.W., Washington, D.C. 20036 or call 1-800-862-5801.

Biggs, Andrew G.
   Social security : the story of its past and a vision for its
   future / Andrew G. Biggs.
      p. cm.
   Includes bibliographical references.
   ISBN-13: 978-0-8447-7208-0 (pbk.)
   ISBN-10: 0-8447-7208-9 (pbk.)
   ISBN-13: 978-0-8447-7209-7 (ebook)
   ISBN-10: 0-8447-7209-7 (ebook)
   1. Social security—United States. I. Title.
   HD7125.B496 2011
   368.4'300973—dc23

CONTENTS

Andrew G. Biggs

LIST OF ILLUSTRATIONS

vii

INTRODUCTION

Social Security is the largest spending program of the federal government, the largest tax paid by most workers, and the largest source of income for most retirees. It pays benefits to Americans, from birth through death, in the form of survivors' benefits for children, disability benefits for working-age individuals, and retirement benefits for older Americans. And it is going broke.

This presents Americans with difficult choices. The decisions we make will depend on both our values and our judgments regarding how to represent those values through policies that are both efficient and consistent with our views regarding individual freedoms and collective responsibilities.

Most articles or books regarding Social Security focus on why the program is going insolvent. This one will be no exception to that rule, although it will present some alternatives to traditional explanations that may be most familiar to readers.

But it is equally important to focus on why Social Security exists in the first place—why we have such a program and what we hope it can accomplish. It is impossible to decide where we wish the program to go over the coming decades until we first understand the multiple and sometimes conflicting goals a national pension program must seek to meet.

As a society we have a moral obligation to care for those who are unable to care for themselves. In addition to theologians and moral philosophers, even thinkers such as Adam Smith, Milton Friedman, and Friedrich von Hayek—economists who are strongly associated with the ideas of free markets and minimal government—believed in a strong safety net for the poor. Social Security provides that lifeline for the low earners, the disabled, and survivors.

However, our duties to the less fortunate notwithstanding, we also have a moral obligation to protect responsible individuals against free riders who would take advantage of generosity to the poor. That is, generous protections for the poor cause a certain number of people to fail to take responsibility for their own financial situation. A program of universal retirement saving ensures that those who can afford to care for themselves will do so, limiting demands on society to those programs needed to support the truly poor. For most people, Social Security is simply mandatory retirement saving, albeit in a form that is often distant from the way we usually think of saving.

And finally, we have a moral responsibility to ourselves not to give up too much of our freedom of choice in return for a security that government may or may not be able to deliver. This is why the growth of Social Security should be limited in the future and its resources focused on protecting the truly needy. One of the ways we express ourselves as independent beings is through the planning and execution of important decisions in our lives, including financial decisions. How to prepare to support yourself and your family during a retirement that could span decades is probably the most important set of financial decisions an individual will ever make.

Financial decisions are often difficult, and public policy can simplify these decisions and better inform individuals—rich, poor, financially savvy, or new to saving—about the choices they make. Even then, some people will make financial decisions with better outcomes than others. But if we take away all important decisions in the name of preventing all negative financial outcomes, we also take away individuals' free choice, the exercise of which is a distinguishing characteristic of being human.

All of this says that while Social Security's goals should remain unchanged, the ways in which it achieves those goals need to be both modernized for the twenty-first century and personalized to give individuals a greater stake in the program.

This book will argue that aspects of Social Security need to be changed, some radically so. But it will also argue that the founding principles of Social Security continue to make sense, even to people who believe in limiting the size of government and increasing individual responsibility and freedom.

Moreover, the book will argue that in some cases, the government should do more with regard to Social Security—in particular, providing a better minimum benefit for the truly poor, many of whom can fall through the safety net as currently constructed. At the same time, in many cases the government should do less: specifically, Social Security pays billions of dollars in benefits each year to middle- and high-income households who could and should save more for retirement on their own. Social Security should be simplified to better target benefits and to make it easier for Americans to know how much they will receive and how much they need to save on their own.

Although the general reason why we have a Social Security program is widely accepted among policy analysts and economists of all political stripes, the decisions we make in meeting its broad goals will differ from person to person. The choices outlined below will not be shared by everyone; rather, they are designed to present an outline of a reformed Social Security program that serves the system's main policy goals while preserving and enhancing individuals' opportunities to make important decisions regarding their lives.

WHY DO WE HAVE A SOCIAL SECURITY PROGRAM?

Nearly every country on earth sponsors a program that, in many ways at least, resembles the United States' Social Security system. Yet people rarely ask why we have it. Often Social Security is just taken for granted as a large and important government program that is financially tottering but needs to be kept going. But by asking and answering the question of why we have such a program and what we want it to do, we can better decide what changes we should make to keep the system healthy for the twenty-first century.

In the following section I will describe the central goals that Social Security is designed to accomplish. The principal goals of a Social Security—like program are to mandate that all working individuals save at least a portion of their earnings for retirement and to provide insurance against poverty in case of unforeseen circumstances. After describing these main goals, I will discuss several other criteria that influence whether a program will in practice likely be successful.

Goal 1: Require Everyone to Save. Perhaps the single most important function of the Social Security program is simply to ensure that everyone saves at least something for retirement. Social Security is, to be sure, a funny sort of "saving." Your contributions come in the form of a tax you are required to pay; these contributions are not truly saved for your retirement in an account; and what you get out of the program may or may not reflect what you paid in. But in the simple sense of having part of your income deducted in your working years and receiving a retirement benefit in exchange, Social Security resembles other forms of retirement saving.

At first glance, requiring individuals to save seems like an inappropriate imposition on personal freedom. Can't people make their own choices regarding whether to save their income for tomorrow or consume it today? In general, yes, and personal choice is one reason the level of Social Security's mandatory "saving" shouldn't be too high.

But there are good reasons to support at least some level of mandatory retirement saving. Lacking this requirement, some individuals will fail to save adequately, and society will be forced to either let them suffer or to bail them out using public funds. The former choice offends our moral sensibilities, while the latter produces perverse incentives such that those who save responsibly are taxed to provide for the irresponsible. The Nobel Prize–winning economist James Buchanan referred to this situation as the "Samaritan's dilemma."[1] The existence of programs to relieve poverty can encourage individuals to depend on such programs, in turn increasing the number of people in poverty.

By requiring individuals to contribute during their working years, Social Security avoids at least some of these problems. In that sense, mandated saving can be seen as protecting the responsible as well as the shortsighted.

In addition to requiring people to save, Social Security dictates the way these savings may be distributed. Rather than paying out a lump sum at retirement, which some individuals might spend quickly, Social Security pays benefits in the form of an "annuity." Annuities are insurance products that pay a fixed monthly benefit for as long as the individual lives. In this way, annuities provide valuable insurance against outliving your retirement savings. While the typical retiree may live to age 83, there is a 20 percent chance of living to age 90 and a 10 percent chance of living to 95. By paying benefits as an annuity, Social Security insures that people will have a retirement income when they need it the most—when they are too old to return to the workforce.

To the degree that individuals are already saving at responsible levels, the requirement to save through Social Security simply means that they will save less elsewhere. For instance, if required to save more through a Social Security program, they might choose to save less through a 401(k) or other retirement vehicles. But for individuals who aren't saving enough, Social Security requires them to put aside more for retirement. This can be good for them and good for those whom they might otherwise come to rely on later in life.

Goal 2: Insurance against a Variety of Risks. Social Security's second main purpose is to assist people who end up in trouble even if they do save responsibly. In short, Social Security provides insurance against poverty in retirement or when a worker becomes disabled or the breadwinner of the family dies. In the past these goals were accomplished through families and communities, and in many cases they still are. But as Americans moved from farms to cities and extended families gave way to smaller households, the ability to "self-insure" against adverse life events through the family and community was reduced. Social Security plays a limited, but still important, role in assisting those who cannot help themselves in case of these unforeseen circumstances.

For instance, even if everyone saved regularly during their working years, there will be individuals whose earnings are so low that they would be insufficient to fund a decent income in retirement. For these people,

Social Security's progressive benefit formula provides extra benefits, more than their own contributions would be able to produce. In this way, Social Security "insures" against the risk of having low lifetime earnings by supplementing benefits for low-income retirees.

Similarly, Social Security provides protections to workers who become disabled and to the families of a deceased worker. These insurance protections resemble life insurance and disability insurance offered in private markets.

There is, of course, a moral element to the goal of reducing poverty. Nearly all religious traditions and moral philosophies hold that we have an obligation to assist those who are unable to help themselves. The Hebrew word "tzedakah," for instance, is often translated as "charity" but in fact denotes something more, an obligation on the part of those who can help to actually do so. Christians are likewise ordered "to look after orphans and widows in their distress" (James 1:27).

There is also an element of prudence. Ideally, people would wish to insure against the chance that some factor outside of their own control would significantly reduce their lifetime earnings. However, private insurance markets fail to provide policies offering these kinds of protections. This is due to something known as "adverse selection," in which people who are more likely to need a form of insurance are also more likely to purchase it. This drives up the price of the insurance, making it even less attractive to ordinary people. The government, by making participation in Social Security universal, can reduce the effects of adverse selection and thereby provide lifetime earnings insurance across the population.

Now, this is not to imply that Social Security's progressivity comes at no cost. Low-income individuals have less incentive to save because Social Security provides them with a supplement to their retirement income; they also have less incentive to increase their incomes because as their lifetime earnings rise, the supplement declines. To the degree that low earnings are caused by factors outside of individuals' control, this will not be a factor. But insofar as individuals can determine their own earnings through education and effort, the protections offered by Social Security's progressive benefit formula should be weighed against the negative incentives they foster. In other words, a balance must be struck.

ADDITIONAL CRITERIA FOR SUCCESS

Any public pension plan should satisfy the above goals of requiring saving, assisting those too poor to save, and protecting against the risk of outliving your assets or leaving your household indigent in the case of disability or death. But a program that satisfies these goals should meet two additional criteria.

First, it should be financially sustainable. That is, it should be reasonably expected that the underlying economy will be able to support these benefits and that the covered population will be willing to do so. More specifically, the level of pension spending depends on the health of the economy and people's willingness to both devote the resources to pensions over other government goals and to government goals in general over private use of their incomes. This sustainable level of spending will differ from country to country and from time to time within a given country and reflect value judgments regarding the appropriate division between public and private use of national resources.

There is no single simple solution to the level of taxes and benefits that will make the program financially sustainable. But we can agree that policymakers and citizens should be good stewards of the Social Security program. For instance, they should balance the burdens and the benefits of the system fairly between rich and poor. Likewise, they should balance the program between current and future generations, not enriching current beneficiaries but leaving future participants worse off. Similarly, good stewardship implies working promptly to fix problems with the program so the problems do not grow and become insurmountable for future generations.

One fact is clear: Social Security as currently structured is financially *unsustainable*. The program's cost currently amounts to around 12.4 percent of the total wage base, or 4.8 percent of gross domestic product. As the baby boom generation retires, life spans increase, and fewer new workers enter the labor force, Social Security's costs will rise while its tax income remains relatively stable. Over the course of the next several decades, the program's growth, without changes in program policy or increases in federal revenues, would generate significant increases in federal deficits and the national debt. That cannot go on forever. Society, working through its elected representatives, must come to some agreement about how to balance Social Security's call on resources with other needs.

Second, the pension plan should provide its benefits in a way that is clear and understandable to participants. This is particularly important in a plan such as Social Security, which is supposed to be one leg of a "three-legged stool" of retirement income that is also composed of employer-sponsored pensions and personal savings. If public pension benefits make up only part of people's total retirement income, they must make their own decisions regarding whether to participate in an employer-sponsored plan and how much to save for retirement on their own. So it is not enough that we have a system that more or less "works." It should also work in a way that is understandable to individuals such that they can make responsible choices regarding their personal saving. If not, retirement security as a whole may suffer even under a perfectly designed Social Security program.

In order to see how to make the system successful, we first need to understand how it currently works and in what specific areas it needs to be reformed. We will turn to those issues next and then address how those reforms might be achieved.

1

**HOW DOES SOCIAL
SECURITY WORK?**

Social Security is designed to meet relatively simple goals, yet the complexities of life—as well as policymakers' desire to fine-tune details and favor certain groups over others—lead to a relatively complex program. This chapter provides basic details on how Social Security functions in practice.

THE BENEFIT FORMULA

It is important to understand the process by which Social Security benefits are calculated, both to better understand the program itself and to comprehend how the complexity of the benefit formula can raise policy issues down the road.

In general terms, Social Security pays a progressive replacement of your average preretirement earnings. While higher earners receive higher benefits in dollar terms, Social Security pays low earners benefits equal to a higher percentage of their preretirement earnings. This means that replacement rates—the Social Security benefit relative to earnings before retirement—are higher for low earners than high earners.

However, benefits can differ based on a number of factors. For example, benefits are adjusted based on when you retire. The standard benefit is paid as of the "full retirement age," which is currently 66 and moving gradually to 67. If you file your claim before the full retirement age, you receive a reduced monthly benefit check, and your monthly benefit rises the longer you delay filing. Claiming at age 62, which is the earliest eligibility age, reduces benefits by around 25 percent.

In general, retirees receive around the same lifetime benefits regardless of when they claim. Claiming earlier means a lower benefit for a larger number of years, while delaying retirement means a higher benefit collected over fewer years. But many experts think that delaying retirement makes sense. Why? The reason is that even if the average 65-year-old lives to age 83, there's a very good chance of living longer—often much longer. One in four 65-year-olds will survive to age 90, and 1 in 10 will live to age 95. A higher Social Security benefit is a way to guarantee a decent standard of living at an age in which you can't easily return to work.

There are other ways in which your Social Security benefit can vary. One important way is Social Security's spousal benefits, which guarantee that the lower-earning spouse receives a benefit that is at a minimum equal to half that of the higher-earning spouse. For instance, if Mr. Smith's benefit was $2,000 per month, but Mrs. Smith's lower earnings qualified her for a benefit of only $500 per month, the spousal benefit would top her up to a total benefit of $1,000. Spousal benefits can increase retirement incomes for many couples, but analysts often argue that they aren't well targeted. For instance, the nonworking spouse of a high-income earner might receive a higher benefit than a low-income woman who worked and contributed her entire life. To address this inequity, some people have called for capping spousal benefits for high-income households.

AVERAGE SOCIAL SECURITY BENEFIT

WORKER	XXXXXXXXXXXXXXXXXXXXXXXXXXXXXXXXXXXXXXXXXXXXXXXX
WIDOW	XXXXXXXXXXXXXXXXXXXXXXXXXXXXXXX
DISABILITY	XXXXXXXXXXXXXXXXXXXX
OVERALL	XXXXXXXXXXXXXXXXX

$1,000	$1,040	$1,080	$1,120	$1,160	$1,200

After benefit claiming, benefits are increased each year based on increases in the Consumer Price Index (CPI). If the CPI increases from the prior year, each January a Cost-of-Living Adjustment (COLA) is paid to Social Security beneficiaries. If prices decline, no COLA is paid until the price level recovers. COLAs are designed to protect retirees against the effects of inflation on the purchasing power of their benefits.

According to the Social Security Administration, the average retired worker benefit as of January 2011 was $1,177. The average widow's benefit was $1,109, and the average disability benefit was $1,068. Overall, the average Social Security benefit as of July 2009 was $1,061.

One upshot of the Social Security benefit formula replacing preretirement earnings is that benefits for new retirees tend to rise over time. If wages rise over time—as they usually do—and if Social Security provides a steady replacement of worker's preretirement income, then Social Security benefits will rise over time as well. That is, a new retiree next year will receive benefits that are higher than those received by retirees this year, and so on into the future.

This means that Social Security reform could reduce the growth of future benefits without actually reducing those benefits to be less than what today's retirees receive. A cut in the growth of benefits would mean that people would need to save more on their own to make up for those reductions. But it wouldn't mean that more people would be thrown into poverty, because the real buying power of benefits—especially for low earners—could continue to rise.

FINANCING

Since its inception, Social Security has been financed as an independent program, with its own dedicated tax spent only on Social Security benefits and administration. (The question of whether the Social Security trust fund has been "raided" will be discussed below.) Social Security's tax began in 1935 as 2 percent of the first $3,000 in earnings. Over time, both the rate and the maximum taxable wage have risen, as shown in igure 1. Today, Social Security is financed by a tax of 12.4 percent on earned income. This tax is nominally split between employers and employees, with each paying 6.2 percent. However, most economists believe that employees effectively pay the full 12.4 percent tax, as employers reduce workers'

FIGURE 1. HISTORICAL EMPLOYEE AND EMPLOYER COMBINED SOCIAL SECURITY PAYROLL TAX RATE

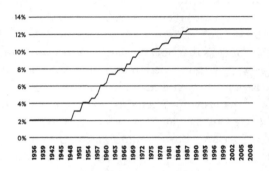

wages to account for the employer share of the tax. (Note that the Obama administration recently cut employees' share of the payroll tax to 4.2 percent, effectively reducing the total Social Security tax withholding rate to 10.4 percent under the Tax Relief, Unemployment Insurance Reauthorization and Job Creation Act of 2010. However, this is only a temporary measure for 2011 aimed at stimulating an economy struggling to recover from the 2007–09 recession and is not important to the long-term Social Security financing debate.)

As of 2011 the Social Security payroll tax is levied on earnings up to a maximum of $106,800. This maximum taxable wage—often called the "tax max" —increases each year at the rate of average wage growth. The tax max is the subject of a great deal of policy discussion, since many have proposed lifting it or eliminating it entirely as a way to address Social Security's long-term funding gap.

Over Social Security's history, a varying amount of total wages has been subject to payroll taxes. At the program's inception, slightly more than 90 percent of total earnings were subject to taxes. The original Social Security Act fixed the taxable maximum at a preset dollar amount. As incomes rose and the maximum taxable amount remained the same, the share of total earnings subject to the tax declined. The 1977 amendments

FIGURE 2. SOCIAL SECURITY TAXABLE EARNINGS AS A PERCENTAGE OF TOTAL COVERED EARNINGS

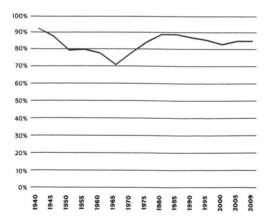

changed the ceiling to increase with average wage growth, and by the early 1980s the ratio had returned to its original level. Over the course of Social Security's history, 84 percent of total earnings have, on average, been subject to payroll taxes, a level comparable to the 85.2 percent estimated average in 2009, as shown in figure 2.

THE PHILOSOPHY BEHIND SOCIAL SECURITY FINANCING

By design, Social Security has not been viewed as a government "welfare program" but as a contributory "social insurance" plan in which benefits are based on a balance between the individual's contributions to the system and the desire to protect low earners. Social Security terms this as a balance between equity and adequacy, between rewarding work and ensuring a decent minimum income. According to the Social Security Administration, the program

> attempts to achieve social adequacy as well as individual equity. The goal of social adequacy assures that individuals receive a level of benefits that reflects their lesser ability to prepare for the risk. The goal of individual equity means that a person receives a reasonable return on his/her investment in Social Security. Thus, while it is true that higher earners receive higher benefits, lower-paid workers receive higher benefits in relation to their earnings in employment

covered by Social Security than do higher-paid workers.[2]

Social Security has always been financed with a flat percentage tax levied on earnings up to a stated maximum. As stated earlier, individuals qualify for benefits based on their past earnings, not based on need. However, benefits are calculated on a progressive basis, meaning that low earners receive higher benefits relative to their contributions than do high earners.

These differences, however, should not be overstated. For instance, a low-earning single male retiring in 2008 could expect to receive a return on his payroll taxes of 2.9 percent above inflation, according to Social Security's actuaries. Returns were 1.9 percent, 1.2 percent, and 0.6 percent for medium, high, and maximum wage earners, respectively.[3] Although significant, the differences in returns between low-wage workers and workers earning the maximum taxable wage are not massive. Although both worker types could expect to receive all their contributions back, the interest rate differences are roughly equivalent to the low-wage worker investing in long-term government bonds and the maximum wage worker holding his money in a passbook savings account. Both are low-risk, low-return investment vehicles.

Some have questioned Social Security's reliance on its own payroll tax rather than being financed out of general tax revenues, meaning principally income taxes. The contributory structure, President Franklin

Roosevelt said, was "politics all the way through. We put those payroll contributions there so as to give the contributors a legal, moral, and political right to collect their pensions and their unemployment benefits. With those taxes in there, no damn politician can ever scrap my social security program. Those taxes aren't a matter of economics, they're straight politics." Roosevelt also specifically mentioned the psychological effect of contributions in destroying the "relief attitude."[4] The 1959 Advisory Council on Social Security similarly stated that "the contribution sets the tone of the program and its administration by making clear that this is not a program of government aid given to the individual, but rather a cooperative program in which the people use the instrument of government to provide protection for themselves and their families against loss of earnings resulting from old age, death and disability."[5]

Likewise, Robert Ball, a former commissioner of Social Security and a defender of the traditional structure of the program, argues that Social Security's funding structure distinguishes it from other government programs: "Social Security is more than a statutory right; it is an *earned* right, with eligibility for benefits and the benefit rate based on an individual's past earnings. This principle sharply distinguishes Social Security from welfare and links the program, appropriately, to other earned rights such as wages, fringe benefits, and private pensions."[6]

As Luke 10:7 says, "The worker deserves his wages."

Likewise, 2 Thessalonians 3:10 says that "if a man shall not work, neither shall he eat." This is not to say that individuals and government programs should not assist those who cannot work, but there is nevertheless a special value placed on earned benefits.

Again, the balance between individual equity and social adequacy is a key to preserving Social Security's standing as distinct from traditional "welfare programs" that are seen as simply transferring resources from higher- to lower-income individuals.

THE SOCIAL SECURITY TRUST FUND

Very little in Social Security policy generates as much controversy as the Social Security trust fund.[7] Many people argue that the Social Security trust fund is as good as gold, a binding commitment backed by the full faith and credit of the United States government. Others argue that the trust fund is a false promise, a phantom fund filled with paper IOUs.

The former view is based on the idea that government bonds held in the trust fund are the same as bonds issued to Wall Street, foreign governments, or ordinary Americans. These bonds are backed by the full faith and credit of the federal government, which has never defaulted on its debt. They are as sure to be paid back as any other investment in the world.

The latter view of the fund is based on the issue of *how* the trust fund's bonds will be paid back and *who* will do the paying. For instance, the Obama administration's fiscal year 2010 budget says that trust fund balances

> are available for future benefit payments and other trust fund expenditures, but only in a bookkeeping sense. The holdings of the trust funds are not assets of the Government as a whole that can be drawn down in the future to fund benefits. Instead, they are claims on the Treasury. From a cash perspective, when trust fund holdings are redeemed to authorize the payment of benefits, the Department of the Treasury finances the expenditure in the same way as any other Federal expenditure—by using current receipts or by borrowing from the public. The existence of large trust fund balances, therefore, does not, by itself, increase the Government's ability to pay benefits. Put differently, these trust fund balances are assets of the program agencies and corresponding liabilities of the Treasury, netting to zero for the Government as a whole.[8]

The first view says that the trust fund is "real" in the sense that it's a solid asset to Social Security. The latter view says the trust fund isn't real because it's an equal and opposite obligation to the rest of the government and thus to the taxpayer. Both views are correct, but both also miss a third, subtler economic point. The trust fund *could* be real, but in practice most economists believe it has turned out not to be.

To illustrate, consider this example: Social Security runs a surplus in a given year of $100 billion. The government issues $100 billion in bonds to Social Security and then uses the $100 billion in cash to pay down existing government debt. Although the government must repay the Social Security bonds in the future, it is better able to do so because the debt it owes to others has been reduced. Put in economic terms, if the $100 billion surplus is used to repay debt, then the amount of capital available in the economy increases and can be invested in tools, factories, computers, and so forth. This increased investment makes workers more productive, which boosts economic growth, workers' wages, and tax revenues. Thus, although the government must repay the trust fund's bonds in the future, the economy will be stronger as a result of today's Social Security surpluses and so will be able to bear that burden without making future workers worse off than they otherwise would have been.

The question is, does this actually happen? Well, we know that the federal government hasn't been repaying any of its outstanding debt lately—much the opposite, in fact. But the trust fund could still benefit the budget and the economy if it reduced the amount the rest of the government needed to borrow. For instance, if the rest of the government would otherwise have borrowed $200 billion in a year, but, thanks to a $100 billion Social Security surplus, it now borrows only $100 billion, we can say that the trust fund improved the budget and likely boosted the economy.

But answering this question demands a counter factual: what would the government have borrowed had Social Security not been running a surplus? At first glance, one would assume that the presence of a Social Security surplus would not affect the size of the deficit in the rest of the budget. But there are several reasons to believe that Social Security surpluses might encourage larger deficits in the rest of the budget. Why?

First, borrowing from Social Security doesn't increase the budget deficit, at least as it is reported in the press. Most news reports discuss the "unified budget" deficit, which means the deficit in the rest of the budget combined with the surplus in Social Security. So if the Social Security surplus increases by one dollar, the rest of the government can increase spending or reduce taxes by one dollar without making the overall budget deficit look worse.

Second, because borrowing from Social Security does not count in the deficit, it also does not increase the reported public debt. Most reports focus on "debt held by the public," meaning borrowing on the open markets, as opposed to "intergovernmental debt" issued to Social Security. Therefore, a dollar borrowed from the private sector counts as real debt, but a dollar borrowed from Social Security is, in practice, largely ignored. Both these factors combined can encourage the rest of the government to take advantage of Social Security surpluses to avoid balancing its books.

Whether this actually occurs is an empirical question but, unfortunately, one whose definitive answer requires us to know what *would* have occurred had Social Security not begun running surpluses from the mid-1980s through today. However, a branch of economics known as econometrics uses statistical techniques to gather information regarding economic activities.

A trio of studies by well-respected economists have concluded that Social Security surpluses since the 1980s have likely *not* translated to improved budget balances. The basic analytical technique is to ask how changes in the Social Security balance correlated with changes to the overall budget balance, after adjusting for other factors. Kent Smetters of the Wharton School, who wrote the first such study, concludes that "there is no empirical evidence supporting the claim that trust fund assets have reduced the level of debt held by the public. In fact, the evidence suggests just the opposite: trust fund assets have probably increased the level of debt held by the public."[9] Barry Bosworth and Gary Burtless of the Brookings Institution, using a sample of Organisation for Economic Co-operation and Development (OECD) countries to supplement results focusing on the United States, conclude:

> A large portion of the accumulation within national social insurance systems is offset for the government sector as a whole by larger

deficits in other budgetary accounts. On average, OECD countries have been able to save only a small portion of any funds accumulated within their social insurance systems in anticipation of large expected liabilities when a growing fraction of the national population is retired. Between 60 and 100 percent of the saving within pension funds is offset by reductions in government saving elsewhere in the public budget.[10]

In other words, a dollar of Social Security surpluses tends to be offset by sixty cents to one dollar in increased spending or reduced taxes in the non–Social Security portion of the budget.

John Shoven of Stanford University and Sita Nataraj of Occidental College examined trust fund saving throughout the federal budget. Their conclusions are summarized as follows: "The authors find a strong negative relationship between the surpluses: an additional dollar of surplus in the trust funds is associated with a $1.50 decrease in the federal funds surplus. This finding is not significantly different from a $1.00 decrease, which would suggest a dollar-for-dollar offset of trust fund surplus with spending increases or tax cuts; the authors are able to reject the hypothesis that the full dollar of trust fund surplus is saved by the government."

In summary, the best evidence suggests that Social Security surpluses, rather than building savings to help pay future Social Security benefits, instead tend to subsidize present consumption. Put another way, Social Security surpluses allow current spending to be higher, or current taxes lower, than they otherwise would be. As Proverbs 20:10 states, "Differing weights and differing measures—the Lord detests them both." It is neither fair to participants in Social Security nor helpful to citizens making policy decisions to have a "trust fund" that doesn't serve as a true store of wealth, as this gives a misleading view of Social Security's financial health and causes some to become unconcerned regarding the need to fix the system's problems.

WHAT DOES IT MEAN TO "SAVE THE SURPLUS"?

"Saving the surplus" can mean that *a dollar of surplus Social Security taxes leads to:*

- *A dollar increase in the Social Security trust fund.* This is the narrowest definition of prefunding, and in this sense the surplus is indisputably "saved." Any surplus taxes are by law used to purchase special-issue Treasury bonds. These bonds carry a market rate of interest and are backed by the full faith and credit of the U.S. government. There is almost no possibility that the government will not honor these bonds, and there are no reform plans that propose that they not be honored.

- *A dollar increase in the overall budget balance.* This is an intermediate level of prefunding, and most advocates of fiscal discipline would be satisfied if this level were achieved. If Social Security's cash balance improves by one dollar and nothing else changes in the rest of the budget, then the overall budget balance will improve by one dollar. Borrowing from the public will be reduced by one dollar (or, if the budget were in surplus, one dollar of existing debt could be repaid). At the least, this level of prefunding makes it easier for the government to repay the Social Security trust fund in the future, because the smaller government debt implies lower annual interest costs.

- *A dollar increase in national saving.* If an additional dollar of Social Security surplus adds to government saving by the above process, and if individuals do not alter their saving behavior, then total saving in the economy will increase by one dollar. This saving adds to the stock of investment capital, such as factories, computers, and so forth, and this additional capital makes future workers more productive and increases economic output. This increased economic output makes it easier to repay the trust fund in the future: wages will be higher, and thus tax receipts will be higher even with a constant tax rate. Thus, we could repay the trust fund without making future workers' after-tax wages lower than they otherwise would have been.

When we talk about "saving the surplus," it makes sense to be clear about which definition of saving we are relying on. The three definitions above are in order of economic value: we would rather that Social Security surpluses improve the overall budget balance than that they only improve Social Security's finances; likewise, it would be better that a Social Security surplus translate to increases in saving and investment in the economy as a whole. Former Obama administration budget chief Peter Orszag and Nobel Prize–winning economist Joseph Stiglitz denote the first definition as "narrow saving," meaning that the reserves of Social Security are increased, but the capacity of the government and the economy to meet Social Security obligations is not improved. "Broad saving," by contrast, implies that the government and the economy's capacity to meet its future obligations rise along with Social Security's trust fund balance.[11]

2

WHY DOES SOCIAL SECURITY NEED REFORM?

One objective of this book is to explain why we have a Social Security program and how it works. But these questions would not be so important to most Americans if the program were not facing financial difficulties. These financing shortfalls mean that reforms to Social Security are inevitable. To make these reforms successful, we need to understand the goals that Social Security seeks to achieve.

But we also need to understand why Social Security faces a funding shortfall in the first place. This chapter will outline two views of the problem. The first is a conventional viewpoint that is understood by many Americans, and the second is newer, involving what is called the "legacy debt." We will then discuss another major problem with the system: the costs incurred by the program being so complex. Understanding all these problems can provide greater insight into the challenges facing Social Security and the steps needed to reform it.

CONVENTIONAL WISDOM: DEMOGRAPHICS

There's a familiar story as to why Social Security is going broke. Basically this story holds that retirees are living longer and families are having fewer children, which means more people collecting benefits and fewer taxpayers to support them. This view contains a good deal of truth, but it is also incomplete.

Social Security is, for all intents and purposes, a "pay-as-you-go program." This means that benefits received by today's retirees, disabled individuals, and survivors are financed directly from taxes paid by today's workers. Unlike a "funded" pension plan, which builds up savings today to help pay benefits in the future, Social Security is simply a transfer program from workers to beneficiaries.

Pay-as-you-go financing makes analysis of the effects of demographic change relatively simple. A program that transfers funds from workers to beneficiaries is affected by the ratio of contributing workers to beneficiaries drawing out of the system.

What demographic changes are we talking about here? First, fertility rates have declined significantly since the baby boom of the 1950s and 1960s. As a result, Americans are having smaller families, and smaller families today mean fewer workers to support Social Security tomorrow. From 1946 through 1960, the fertility rate averaged 3.34 children per woman, meaning that the typical woman would have that many children over her lifetime. Since then, however, fertility rates have fallen to around 2 children per woman and are expected to remain in that range in the future.[12]

Second, life expectancies have increased since Social Security was founded. More working-age Americans survive to retirement, and those who do reach retirement age live longer than did Americans in the past. For instance, according to the Social Security Administration, in 1940 a 21-year-old man had a 53.9 percent chance of surviving to age 65 and from there had a typical life expectancy of an additional 12.7 years. By

1990, the chance of surviving to 65 had risen to 72.3 percent, and life expectancy as of age 65 had risen to 15.3 years.[13] Women experienced even larger increases in life expectancies during this period. This implies more retirees collecting benefits for a longer time.

Today's retirees have also lengthened their retirements by beginning retirement earlier. Despite the increasing normal retirement age, the claiming age has declined over time. The average age of Social Security benefit claiming has fallen from 68.4 in 1955 and 65.7 in 1965 to 63.6 in 2008.[14]

Combined, lower fertility rates, higher life expectancies, and shorter working lives imply fewer workers and more beneficiaries. Over the next two decades, America's population will add many more

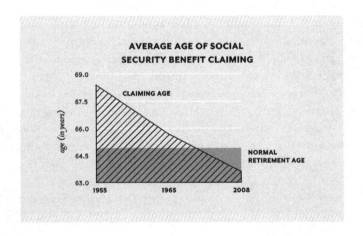

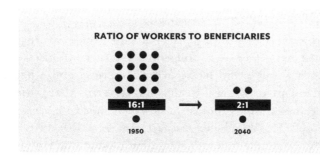

RATIO OF WORKERS TO BENEFICIARIES

16:1 → 2:1

1950   2040

retirees than it will working-age individuals to support them. In simple terms, when the worker-beneficiary ratio declines, the burden of supporting each beneficiary is divided up among fewer workers.

When the ratio of workers to beneficiaries is high, as it was in the past, Social Security benefits are easy to finance. In 1950, for instance, there were 16.5 workers per beneficiary. On this basis, we could have financed full benefits with a tax rate of around 2.2 percent. As it happens, in 1950 the total Social Security payroll tax rate was 2 percent, showing that the system was right around balance at the time.

Now, what happens when the ratio of workers to beneficiaries declines? Assuming the ratio of benefits to average wages stays the same, the cost to each worker must rise. If the worker-to-beneficiary ratio drops to 2 to 1, as it will by the 2040s, then the cost of paying full benefits at today's levels would rise to around 18 percent of wages.

The main demographic shift will occur over the next

several decades, as the massive baby boom generation shifts from their working years—in which their earnings swelled tax coffers—to retirement, when they will instead begin drawing on Social Security, Medicare, and other government programs. In the longer term, rising life expectancies will produce a slow but steady increase in costs. This highlights the fact that Social Security's financing problems aren't a one-time event due simply to the baby boom generation such that when the baby boomers die the program will return to solvency. Rather, the retirement of the baby boomers simply speeds up a general process of population aging that is expected to continue indefinitely. There is no point at which Social Security's problems can be expected to fix themselves. Rather, it is up to us to fix them.

Yet, while demographics tell a compelling story, they do not tell the complete story. Consider this fact: on average, each worker now paying into Social Security will pay more than enough in taxes to finance the benefits they will be owed in retirement. The same goes for future workers. If each worker is paying enough to fund his own benefits, how can it be that Social Security faces multi-trillion-dollar shortfalls? To answer that question, we must turn from the future to the past.

ALTERNATE VIEW: LEGACY DEBT

As stated above, on an individual basis Americans are paying more than enough in taxes to finance their own benefits. For instance, individuals born in 1960—and therefore retiring in the mid-2020s—will on average pay taxes that are 25 percent more than is needed to finance their benefits.

If that's the case, how can Social Security possibly be going bankrupt? The answer is that while current and future participants will pay more than enough to finance their own benefits, past and many present retirees didn't pay nearly enough. These early participants in the Social Security program received benefits vastly in excess of the taxes they paid. This overhang—often referred to as a "legacy debt"—has sapped the contributions of current workers, leaving the program without enough to cover them once they reach retirement.

A pay-as-you-go program has one significant advantage over a fully funded program: it can begin paying benefits immediately, whereas a funded program cannot begin paying full benefits until participants have paid into the program for a full working lifetime. When the Social Security Act was initially passed in 1935, a compromise approach was taken: benefits would start being paid in 1944, but it would be longer before retirees received full benefit payments. This would have more closely followed the pattern of a funded pension plan, and the Social Security trust fund would have built up significant reserves as workers began paying into the system.

The 1939 amendments to the Social Security Act changed all that. Benefit payments were moved forward to 1940, and scheduled tax increases, which would have further increased the trust fund, were delayed. In addition, the benefit formula was changed so that new retirees could receive more or less full benefits even though they had paid into the program for only a few years. As a result, Social Security became the "pay-as-you-go" program that we know today. Only small trust fund reserves were built up, and even that was only to smooth small year-to-year fluctuations in revenues and benefit payments.

The result of these changes was that Social Security was an incredibly good deal for early generations of retirees. Because they received full retirement benefits while having paid only a few years of taxes into the program, and even these at a low tax rate of 2 percent of their earnings, most participants received far more in benefits than they paid in taxes. The first Social Security retiree, Ida Mae Fuller, paid $25.00 in taxes but collected

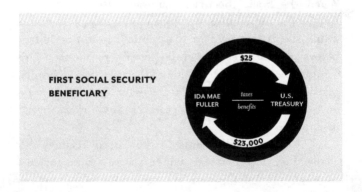

FIRST SOCIAL SECURITY BENEFICIARY

more than $23,000 in benefits.

The generation retiring in 1950 received on average 16 times more in benefits than they paid in taxes. That amounts to an average annual return on their payroll taxes of 30 percent. In 1965—fully 30 years after the program began—retirees still received an average of 12 times more in benefits than they paid in taxes. Even the cohort retiring in 1985 received a return of around 7 percent above inflation, the same as on stocks but with none of the risk. Overall, past and current participants have collected around $17 trillion more in Social Security benefits than they paid in taxes.

Because the total benefits paid out by Social Security must ultimately equal the total taxes it collects, if past participants in Social Security received $17 trillion more than they paid in, future participants must receive $17 trillion less.

Social Security's trustees report that the system faces a long-term shortfall of around $15 trillion. That means that if the Social Security trust fund had an additional $15 trillion in it today, the system could pay full promised benefits in perpetuity. Now, had past and present beneficiaries received back only what they paid in, plus interest at the government bond rate, the trust fund would be around *$17 trillion* larger today than it is. A total trust fund balance of close to $20 trillion would be more than enough to keep the system solvent in perpetuity. So the stories about greedy baby boomers sucking the system dry are basically false;

these folks are more than paying their way. In fact it was the so-called greatest generation that collected more than they paid.

Now, how does this legacy debt view of Social Security's solvency relate to the demographic story? Both are true. If, say, fertility rose so the future population was bigger, we could divide that $17 trillion up among a larger number of people. Or if the economy grew faster, then that $17 trillion would be smaller relative to our earnings. Or if people didn't live as long as expected, Social Security would be a worse deal to them, and so we could repay part of the $17 trillion out of benefits these folks wouldn't receive. But none of this tells us how the Social Security deficit was generated in the first place: that was entirely a function of paying early generations far, far more in benefits than they contributed in taxes.

In addition to understanding how the Social Security shortfall was generated, the legacy debt story tells us something else: that it will be very hard to solve. Excess payments to early beneficiaries were made, and we can't get the money back. Maybe it was a good idea to pay generous benefits when Social Security started, and maybe it wasn't. But we've inherited the legacy debt, and our task now is to determine how to resolve it in a way that not only is fair to current and future participants but also helps the Social Security program continue to achieve its goals.

THE COSTS OF COMPLEXITY

I have explained how a universal, progressive, defined-benefit Social Security program can provide valuable social insurance protections that private markets may not cover. But advantages in theory won't necessarily play out in practice. This section outlines how Social Security often falls short and why.

The principal problem examined in this section is complexity. The Social Security benefit formula is far more complicated and detailed than most people realize. This complexity imposes two related costs on Social Security participants. First, the benefit formula makes it difficult for a typical individual to know in advance what he or she will receive from the program. This makes planning other retirement saving more difficult. Second, the complexity of the benefit formula implies that individuals and households with identical lifetime earnings and contributions to the program often receive very different levels of benefits. This undermines the social insurance value of the program, because low earners who need additional benefits may not always receive them.

Why are Social Security benefits so hard to predict? The advantage of a traditional "defined benefit" pension over "defined contribution" plans like 401(k)s is supposed to be predictability—that you know what you're going to get. A private sector defined-benefit pension provides that predictability: the benefit is usually equal to a percentage of a worker's final salary multiplied by the number of years the worker has on the job. For instance, a benefit might equal 1 percent of final salary times the number of years of service. Innumerate though many Americans may be, this remains an easy calculation to carry out, allowing workers to form reasonably accurate expectations of their future retirement income.

But corporate pensions' relative simplicity definitely does *not* translate over to Social Security's benefit formula. Here's how Social Security benefits are actually calculated. First, a worker's past earnings are indexed to the growth of average national wages. This involves multiplying the ratio of earnings in a past year to average wages economy-wide in that year by the average wage in the year the worker turned sixty. Earnings past age sixty are not indexed.

Next, Social Security averages the highest thirty-five years of indexed earnings. These average earnings are then run through a progressive benefit formula to produce the Primary Insurance Amount payable at the full retirement age, currently 66. For a new retiree in 2009, Social Security replaces 90 percent of the first $744 in average monthly earnings, 32 percent of earnings between $745 and $4,483, and 15 percent of earnings above $4,483. However, if this benefit is less than half of the benefit received by the higher-earning spouse in a married couple, the lower-earning spouse is eligible to receive a spousal benefit instead. Spousal benefits may be collected off the earnings record of a former spouse, but only if the marriage lasted at least ten years.

The resulting benefit is then reduced or increased based on whether benefits are claimed before or after the full retirement age. Finally, the retirement earnings test, a provision imposed on early claimants who continue working, may reduce benefits. Few Americans are aware, however, that at the full retirement age, benefits are recalculated to account for benefits lost earlier to the earnings test.

In short, this is not the sort of calculation someone can do in his head. The complexity of the calculations required makes it almost impossible for individuals to know in advance what they will receive from the program. But, as stated above, advance knowledge of benefits allows individuals to make more informed decisions regarding how much they will save and how long they will choose to work. A simple, predictable Social Security benefit should allow working-age individuals to decide how much to save through individual retirement accounts (IRAs), 401(k) plans, or other vehicles. If Social Security benefits themselves are too hard to predict, these tasks become much harder.

How bad is the problem? Using the Health and Retirement Study, a federally funded survey of older Americans, I compared near-retirees' predictions of their future Social Security benefits to what those benefits actually turned out to be at retirement. I found first that almost one quarter of near-retirees would not even hazard a guess as to their future "defined benefit." It is difficult to imagine how effectively these individuals could plan for retirement without having any idea how much they would receive from Social Security.

Then, of those who could make a prediction, one-third overestimated their benefits by at least 10 percent, and one-quarter overestimated them by more than 28 percent. One in ten retirees received a benefit less than half as much as they expected. Similar numbers underestimated their future benefits. Put simply, a significant portion of Americans have no idea what their supposedly predictable Social Security benefit will be until the first check arrives. By this time, of course, it is too late to do much about it.

The second problem is also related to the complexity in the benefit formula. One of the advantages of a mandatory Social Security program is that, through a progressive benefit formula, it can protect individuals

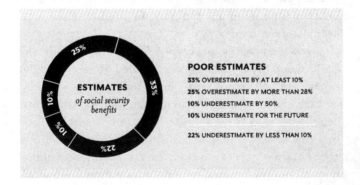

ESTIMATES *of social security benefits*

25%
33%
10%
10%
22%

POOR ESTIMATES

33% OVERESTIMATE BY AT LEAST 10%
25% OVERESTIMATE BY MORE THAN 28%
10% UNDERESTIMATE BY 50%
10% UNDERESTIMATE FOR THE FUTURE

22% UNDERESTIMATE BY LESS THAN 10%

who have had low lifetime wages. That's the insurance function of Social Security.

In this vein, University of Oregon economist Mark Thoma argues that Social Security is fundamentally an insurance program:

> It is no different than fire insurance. Without such insurance, people would need to save enough to replace their homes should a fire break out. All risk must be borne individually, and most people end up saving far more than needed compared to an insurance program providing identical benefits. Others are left without any protection at all. With fire insurance, each person pays a smaller amount into a fund, and those unlucky few who need the insurance collect. There is no expectation that the amount paid in and the amount collected will necessarily match. Social Security insurance is no different.[15]

This is a legitimate point. However, to satisfy this insurance function, it is not enough that Social Security be progressive *on average*. To be truly effective, the Social Security program must be *reliably* progressive. Just as homeowners' insurance would be less valuable if the policy was uncertain to pay off in the event of a fire, Social Security's implicit wage insurance becomes less valuable if low earners do not receive consistently higher replacement rates than higher earners.

The progressivity of the basic formula for calculating the basic retirement benefits dictates that replacement rates should be higher for individuals with lower lifetime earnings. However, there are a number of ways in which individuals with the same lifetime earnings can receive significantly different benefits. For instance, Social Security benefits are based only on a worker's highest 35 years of earnings; therefore, two individuals with the same total lifetime earnings could receive very different benefits if one compressed those earnings into 30 years of work while the other spread them over 40 years. Likewise, Social Security pays spousal benefits when one spouse has earnings much lower than the other. Thus, a couple in which one spouse works outside the home while the other does not would receive higher benefits than a couple with the same total household earnings but where each spouse worked and had the same salary. Other facets of the benefit formula also result in households with similar earnings and payments into the program receiving different benefits at retirement.

The result is that many low-earning households fail to receive truly adequate benefits, while other households receive relatively generous benefits that they may not need. This is akin to an insurance policy that may or may not pay off if your house burns down—which is to say, a not very reliable insurance policy. These differences are due to quirks in the benefit formula, which Social Security reform could and should address.

Reform should ensure that low-earning households reliably receive more generous benefits, relative to their preretirement earnings, than do higher-earning households. Such reforms would make Social Security a "social insurance" program that can be relied on.

3

HOW SHOULD WE FIX
SOCIAL SECURITY?

Given all that has been discussed above, how should the Social Security program be amended for the future? This chapter begins with general outlines and then sums up what a reformed Social Security system might look like.

SEPARATING LEGACY COSTS FROM ONGOING COSTS

As discussed above, if it were not for overpayments to earlier generations of participants—the so-called legacy debt—Social Security would be solvent for the future, notwithstanding the aging of the population. Because this legacy debt is financed alongside the ordinary running costs of the program, however, perceptions of the cause of Social Security's shortfalls and the value offered by the system can be skewed.

There is no "solution" that will simply erase the legacy debt; those overpayments were made beginning decades ago and cannot be reclaimed. Those early participants were made better off by those payments, and current and future participants are made worse off. Although it is interesting to argue whether this transfer made sense, these debates cannot alter the fact that it has already happened and cannot be undone.

However, we can consider the pros and cons of different ways of servicing and repaying this debt. Under current law, the servicing of the legacy debt is combined with Social Security contributions that are repaid in full as retirement, disability, and survivors benefits. In other words, part of the Social Security payroll tax is what economists call a "pure tax," which services the legacy debt and for which nothing is received in return, and part is a "contribution" that individuals can expect to receive back in full, plus interest, through their benefits.

One problem with this is that individuals come to see Social Security as a poor deal because a good part of what they pay into the program gets them nothing in return. As a result, they tend to become more skeptical about the Social Security system as a whole.

One potential solution to this problem is to levy separate taxes to fund Social Security's legacy costs and its ongoing costs. Social Security's contributory structure almost requires that future benefits be based on a tax on wages today, because otherwise the crucial link between what is paid and what is received is lost. But Social Security's legacy costs can be financed with any sort of tax.

Peter Diamond and Peter Orszag, for instance, propose financing part of the legacy debt through a 3 percent tax on all earnings above the Social Security maximum taxable wage, currently $106,800.[16] Likewise, Alicia Munnell suggests that Social Security's legacy costs might be financed as any other federal debt would be, using general tax revenues funded by income and other taxes.[17] Of course, these are not the only options available. Some have proposed, for instance, a carbon tax to reduce the threat of global climate change. Others have discussed introducing a so-called Value Added Tax, a form of national sales tax. Revenues from either of these could be dedicated to funding

Social Security's legacy costs.

The broad point is that while an individual's entitlement to future Social Security benefits should be based on the contributions he or she makes to the program, the legacy debt can be funded in whatever way policymakers decide is fairest and most efficient. That allows considerable flexibility to design funding sources that will minimize the negative effects of taxes on work effort and savings. Now, economists do not universally agree on what the best tax system might be, so simply deciding to fund Social Security's legacy costs outside of the current payroll tax does not by itself determine how it might be done. But it does allow for a broader debate on how this cost might be borne.

UNIVERSAL RETIREMENT SAVING ACCOUNTS

Recall that Social Security's first and largest goal is to require individuals to save a portion of their earnings for retirement to reduce the chance that individuals who fail to plan ahead will need to rely on others for a retirement income. But if mandating retirement saving is the goal, there is a way that is simpler, more efficient, and more consistent with individual freedom than forcing individuals to pay a payroll tax that flows to the government, may or may not be saved in a trust fund, and is then repaid via a benefit formula that is often arbitrary and difficult to understand.

That alternative to saving through Social Security is simply to mandate retirement saving through widely available savings vehicles such as 401(k) plans or individual retirement accounts. Much of what Social Security was founded to do could be accomplished if each working American were offered a retirement savings account and chose to participate in it.

In addition, if everyone saved a reasonable amount for retirement, Social Security could focus its resources on low-income households that need them the most. If we chose, Social Security could provide every retired and disabled household a poverty-level benefit for less than half of what we currently spend on the program. One reason we can't follow this path is that Social Security provides significant benefits to many middle- and high-earning households. There is a good reason for this—President Roosevelt wanted Social Security to be a universal benefit rather than a targeted "welfare program" —but the costs of paying benefits to households that face little danger of poverty in retirement are nevertheless growing larger.

This is compounded by the fact that many American households—in particular middle- and high-income households—save less on their own because of the existence of Social Security benefits. The Congressional Budget Office reviewed the academic literature and found that the typical household reduced its savings by up to 50 cents for each dollar it expected to receive from Social Security.[18] So, at least in part, Social Security causes part of the problem it seeks to address. If we could increase individual retirement saving, Social Security's job would be easier, and the cost of accomplishing its goal would be reduced.

Today, most employers offer 401(k) or similar retirement accounts. In these cases the important issue is how to get individuals to participate. Until recently, the only direct incentive was the employer match of employee contributions. Although this should be enough to get most employees to participate, research shows that employer matches are actually not very effective in encouraging workers to save.[19]

Likewise, tax incentives for retirement saving do little for low- and middle-income individuals. Under current law, contributions to 401(k) and IRA accounts are deductible from income taxes. Taxes are paid only when funds are withdrawn from accounts in retirement. But most low- and middle-income households pay little or no income taxes after a variety of tax credits and deductions are included. This means that they receive little tax benefit from contribution to a retirement account. This also doubtless contributes to reduced participation by low- and middle-income households.

An alternate approach, which has grown more popular in recent years, is to automatically enroll all new employees in a firm's retirement plan. Until recently, only individuals who affirmatively chose to participate would be enrolled. Human nature being what it is, many people simply fail to get around to it. If everyone is automatically enrolled, however, inertia works to the savers' advantage. Individuals who truly wish not to take part can withdraw, but those who simply "go with the flow" will at least begin amassing savings for retirement. Automatic enrollment can double or triple participation rates among women, minorities, and workers with low incomes—all of whom have low participation rates under current rules.[20]

Many employers—particularly small- and medium-sized firms—do not offer retirement savings plans, making automatic enrollment impossible. These businesses often cite the complexity and regulatory costs of retirement plans under current law, which can be significant. In response, Eugene Steuerle and Pamela Perun have suggested a "super simple" retirement savings plan designed to reduce administrative burdens on employers through a simple, low-cost account structure.[21] This approach could help to make retirement savings vehicles available to every working American.

It remains to be seen how successful these types of reforms may be. Already, over one-third of firms are automatically enrolling employees in 401(k) accounts, which will increase the number of savers nationwide. But it remains the case that individuals whose employers fail to automatically enroll them—or individuals who are enrolled but then choose to withdraw from a retirement plan—may be among the most vulnerable to poverty in old age.

For this reason, we should keep on the table the option to make retirement saving truly universal by making it mandatory. Australia has already done so.

Beginning in the early 1990s, all employees were required to save 9 percent of their wages in individual retirement accounts managed by their employers. These accounts are managed similarly to 401(k) plans. The government's role is to provide a backstop benefit for low-income retirees whose account assets and other savings are insufficient to reach a stated minimum level. This approach has not been perfect in practice, but Australia has shown that government can restrict itself to requiring retirement saving while leaving the saving itself to individuals and the private sector.

FLAT BENEFIT FOR LOW EARNERS

The second main function of Social Security— supplementing the savings of low earners—is one that can only effectively be done by government. Private sector insurance against low lifetime earnings is not available, and the charitable sector can only be expected to do so much. But, as shown above, the safety net provided by Social Security has many holes.

One approach for strengthening the safety net would be to simplify it: instead of a complex benefit formula dictating different benefits for different types of beneficiaries, the program would simply pay a flat dollar benefit to every qualifying retiree household. This approach—which is sometimes referred to as a "universal pension"—has most prominently been used in New Zealand, though a number of developing countries have also adopted it.[22]

New Zealand pays all individuals age 65 and over who have met a residency test a basic pension benefit that is equal to around 40 percent of the average wage among working-age residents. This level is roughly comparable to the average benefit paid by Social Security, but because the benefit is the same for every retiree, the New Zealand program is significantly more progressive than Social Security.

A flat-benefit approach has both advantages and disadvantages. Relative to Social Security, it can provide a more predictable benefit on which to plan other retirement saving and a surer safety net against poverty. In addition, because a flat benefit provides such a strong safety net, retirement savings on top of it may require less regulation by government.

At the same time, however, a flat benefit has important disadvantages. First, because it severs the link between earnings and retirement benefits, it would depart from Social Security's traditional "earned benefit" approach. And because a flat benefit is more progressive than the current Social Security benefit formula, it might come to be perceived more as a "welfare program" than as contributory social insurance. Finally, because a flat benefit would be paid to all retirees, regardless of how much they worked or saved, we could expect that younger individuals would work and save less in response.

One way to potentially balance these advantages and disadvantages would be to implement a flat dollar benefit but at a lower level than is paid by New Zealand.

On top of that, individuals would prepare for retirement through universal retirement savings accounts. For instance, each retiree household could be provided with a flat payment at the poverty level for a cost of around 5.8 percent of total wages, versus the 12.4 percent of pay that is currently dedicated to Social Security. Social Security would need to fund benefits for working-age disabled individuals and survivors, which would increase costs somewhat.

On top of this, individuals would save to help provide for additional income in retirement. If each individual saved around 3 percent of earnings in a retirement account invested in safe government bonds, total benefits—the flat benefit plus the benefit derived from the account—would be similar to those paid by Social Security today. Moreover, the progressivity of total benefits would also be similar to that under the Social Security program. The main differences would be that the redistributive portion of Social Security would be made explicit through the flat benefit, while the mandatory savings element of Social Security would be implemented through personal saving rather than paid through the government.

There is nothing free in this proposal: although costs to the Social Security program would be lowered by focusing more on a poverty-protection mission, individuals would need to take more responsibility for their retirement saving. Moreover, when the costs of funding Social Security's legacy debt are included, total costs would be similar to those under the current program. As life spans increased, individuals would need to increase their retirement saving during working years. And to build a truly secure retirement, individuals would need to save more because the 3 percent account contribution rate to match Social Security benefit levels would not be sufficient.

But as opposed to traditional proposals to reduce Social Security costs, it would not simply leave the current benefit structure in place but radically reform it to ensure a strong safety net for all retirees while simultaneously increasing emphasis on personal saving.

This approach is consistent with the view that where government action is justified it should be robust, but that government action should be limited to essential functions that cannot be performed by the private sector.

MANDATORY ANNUITIZATION

It is not enough that individuals save sufficiently for retirement; it is also important that those savings be around in their later years. That is why one of the main purposes of Social Security is to protect against longevity risk, that of outlasting your assets through a longer-than-expected lifetime. If Social Security were converted to a flat benefit structure similar to New Zealand's, that characteristic would be retained—benefits would continue for as long as the beneficiary lived.

But if a greater share of retirement income preparation fell on individual saving, the dangers of outliving your assets might increase. Most individuals with 401(k) plans withdraw their savings as lump sums, exposing them to the risk of outliving their assets. Few retirees currently purchase annuities for the purpose of protecting against longevity risks.

Two policies might help protect against longevity risk. First, individuals with personal accounts might be required to use part of their accounts to purchase annuities. But these annuities need not begin at age 65. For instance, individuals might purchase annuities that began payment only at age 85. Most people would not survive to collect, but this would make the annuity cheaper to purchase. Moreover, those who did survive past age 85 would be grateful for having purchased the annuity, because it would help insure them against income needs in extreme old age.

Second, part of the tax funds currently used to encourage retirement saving might be converted to encourage annuitization of retirement savings. Each year the federal government effectively spends more than $100 billion providing a tax exemption for contributions to employer-sponsored pensions and individual retirement accounts. Withdrawals from these accounts, by contrast, are subject to income taxes. As an alternative, some of these incentive funds might be diverted to allow a given portion of 401(k) or IRA balances to remain untaxed if they are converted to an annuity at retirement. The costs of this incentive might be covered by capping the deductibility of retirement account contributions for the highest earners. This approach could potentially produce significant increases in the share of retirement assets that are annuitized, which most economists believe would increase individual welfare and improve retirement security.

WHAT A REFORMED SOCIAL SECURITY PROGRAM MIGHT LOOK LIKE

Here's what a reformed Social Security program might look like.

First, each American would be subject to a dedicated tax designed to cover Social Security's legacy costs. This tax, which could take the form of an explicit part of the existing payroll tax, a consumption tax like a value-added tax, an addition to the income tax, or some other construct, would produce no entitlement to benefits. It would be a "pure tax" designed simply to cover the program's inherited costs.

Second, each worker would automatically be enrolled in a workplace pension plan such as a 401(k). At the least, workers would need to save around 3 percent of their earnings to produce total benefits comparable to those from Social Security. These contributions would be exempt from income taxes. Since Social Security makes up only one part of an individual's total retirement income, default contribution rates should be higher than 3 percent—in the range of 8 to 10 percent of earnings. Although individuals may choose how to allocate their contributions to different investments, as they may do under current law, a default investment in a "life cycle" portfolio, which automatically shifts from stocks to bonds as the worker ages, makes sense. At retirement, a portion of account balance would remain untaxed if it were converted to a life annuity.

Third, each eligible beneficiary would receive a flat dollar benefit equal to the federal poverty guideline. In the future, this flat benefit would increase along with the growth of wages so that the ratio of the flat benefit to benefits derived from personal savings, which would naturally rise with wages, would remain constant. These payments would be made to retirees, survivors, and the disabled.

Eligibility can derive from a number of criteria. New Zealand's flat benefit is almost universal, paying to any individual with 10 years or residency in the country, regardless of labor force participation. Alternately, eligibility could be defined by the number of years an individual has been in the workforce—for instance, individuals might become eligible for a given portion of the benefit for each year they worked. This would retain incentives to work, which otherwise would be weakened by a universal pension, but would also leave holes in the safety net. Most people who are poor in retirement are not so due to low wages during the periods in which they worked but because of infrequent participation in the labor force. The tighter the work qualification, the more likely such individuals would be left behind. Thus, a balance must be struck.

It is also important to decide *when* retirees become eligible for this benefit. In New Zealand, no benefit is payable prior to age 65. In contrast, in the United States, as mentioned earlier, reduced Social Security benefits are payable as early as age 62, even as the full retirement age gradually rises to age 67. However, the availability of Social Security benefits as early as age 62 has encouraged many Americans to retire earlier even as life spans increase and health at older ages improves. In the 1950s the typical retiree claimed Social Security at age 68 and lived only to his mid to late 70s. Today, age 62 is the most common claiming age, even as retirees can expect to live to their early 80s. Thus, many Americans will spend one-third of their adult lives in retirement.

It makes sense to shift back somewhat in terms of benefit-claiming ages. The age of early benefit claiming should be increased to 65, while the age for receiving a full benefit should continue to rise past 67 as life spans increase. Those who delay retirement past the full claiming age should receive increased benefits.

In addition, this reformed program would continue to provide survivors benefits and benefits to disabled workers as the current program does. Survivors benefits should probably be somewhat higher than under current law, as under the current program a widow or widower may see his or her total household benefit cut by one-third to one-half on the death of a spouse, but household expenses fall by much less than that. Disability benefits should be retained, but policymakers should consider tightening eligibility for disability benefits to reduce the growth of costs over time.

What would this new system produce?

Individuals would have greater safety against poverty in old age because of a base benefit that would allow fewer vulnerable Americans to fall through the cracks. At the same time, individual retirement saving would be increased, building retirement assets in a way that is good for the economy and consistent with personal choice. Finally, the legacy tax would recognize the inherited shortfalls of the Social Security program and fund them distinctly from the contributions to the ongoing system. This would provide greater clarity to participants regarding how the system functions and where their money is going.

This amended program would accomplish the main goals of Social Security more effectively than the current system does, but in a way that encourages rather than discourages personal saving and ownership. The program's costs and benefits would be more transparent and easier to understand, such that individuals would have a more accurate perception of what Social Security will provide and what they must provide for themselves. And public faith in the program would be strengthened by the realization that much of the costs that make Social Security a perceived poor deal for younger Americans are part of an inherited debt, not due to waste or theft within the ongoing structure of the program.

CONCLUDING REMARKS

Social Security has a storied past, but without change it faces a troubled future. The program has not saved enough to cover rising costs as the baby boom generation retires, and as a result it could fall short of funds for future generations. But fixing these financial problems isn't just a matter of raising taxes or reducing benefits. Rather, we need to reassess what we wish the program to accomplish and craft policies that can do so in light of twenty-first-century realities.

Social Security policy—and government policy in general—relies on values and execution. Values determine the goals of government policy, and execution determines how well those goals are accomplished. I have argued here that many of Social Security's goals make sense and are consistent with our values. But a better understanding of how Social Security works will assist Americans in making sure the program remains consistent with their values and effective in reaching its goals.

ENDNOTES

1 James M. Buchanan, "The Samaritan's Dilemma," in *Altruism, Morality and Economic Theory*, ed. E. S. Phelps (New York: Russell Sage Foundation, 1975), 71–85.

2 Social Security Administration, "Frequently Asked Questions: How Does It Work?" http://www.ssa.gov/kids/workfacts.htm.

3 See Orlo Nichols, Michael Clingman, Alice Wade, and Chris Chaplain, "Internal Real Rates of Return under the OASDI Program for Hypothetical Workers," Social Security Administration, Actuarial Note 2007.5, November 2007.

4 See Social Security Administration, http://www.ssa.gov/history/Gulick.html.

5 See Department of Health, Education and Welfare, *Financing Old Age, Survivors and Disability Insurance: A Report of the Advisory Council on Social Security Financing* (Washington, DC: U.S. Government Printing Office, 1959).

6 Robert Ball, *The Nine Guiding Principles of Social Security* (New York: Century Foundation, 1998).

7 In fact, there are actually two Social Security trust funds, one for the Old Age and Survivors program and one for the Disability Insurance program, but in most discussions their balances are merged and they are treated as a single entity.

8 See http://www.gpoaccess.gov/usbudget/fy10/pdf/spec.pdf, page 345 of the "Analytical Perspectives" volume of the budget.

9 Kent Smetters, "Is the Social Security Trust Fund Worth Anything?" (NBER Working Paper No. W9845, Cambridge, MA, July 2003), available at http://papers.ssrn.com/sol3/papers.cfm?abstract_id=425581.

10 Barry Bosworth and Gary Burtless, "Pension Reform and Saving" (Brookings Institution, Washington, DC, January 5, 2004), available at http://www.brookings.edu/~/media/Files/rc/papers/2004/0105useconomics_bosworth/200401bosworthburtless.pdf.

11 Peter Orszag and Joseph Stiglitz, "Rethinking Pension Reform: Ten Myths about Social Security Systems" (paper presented at New Ideas about Old Age Security Conference, World Bank, Washington, DC, September 14–15, 1999), available at http://www.ssc.wisc.edu/~scholz/Teaching_742/Orszag-Stiglitz.pdf.

12 According to recent reporting from the Center for Disease Control's National Vital Statistics, total lifetime fertility in 2007 was 2.12 births per woman. This value is just above the general rule of 2.1 births per woman to sustain the current population size. See National Vital Statistics Reports, "Births: Preliminary Data for 2007," March 18, 2009, available at http://www.cdc.gov/nchs/data/nvsr/nvsr57/nvsr57_12.pdf.

13 Social Security Administration, "Life Expectancy for Social Security," http://www.ssa.gov/history/lifeexpect.html.

14 "Annual Statistical Supplement, 2009," *Social Security Bulletin* (February 2006), table 6.B5, available at http://www.socialsecurity.gov/policy/docs/statcomps/supplement/2009/6b.html.

15 Mark Thoma, "Social Security Is about Insurance, Not Savings," *Eugene (OR) Register Guard*, February 24, 2005, available at http://economistsview.typepad.com/economistsview/2005/03/_social_securit.html.

16 See Peter A. Diamond and Peter R. Orszag, "A Summary of Saving Social Security: A Balanced Approach" (MIT Department of Economics Working Paper No. 04-21, May 2004).

17 Alicia H. Munnell, "Should Social Security Rely Solely on the Payroll Tax?" (Center for Retirement Research at Boston College, Brief No. 9-16, 2009).

18 Congressional Budget Office, "Social Security and Private Saving: A Review of the Empirical Evidence" (Congressional Budget Office, Washington, DC, July 1998).

19 Olivia S. Mitchell, Stephen P. Utkus, and Tongxuan Yang, "Turning Workers into Savers? Incentives, Liquidity, and Choice in 401(K) Plan Design" (NBER Working Paper Series, W11726, Cambridge, MA, October 2005).

20 Brigitte C. Madrian and Dennis F. Shea, "The Power of Suggestion: Inertia in 401(k) Participation and Savings Behavior," April 2000.

21 Pamela J. Perun and C. Eugene Steuerle, "Why Not a 'Super Simple' Saving Plan for the United States?" May 2008.

22 Larry Willmore, "Universal Pensions in Low Income Countries" (Initiative for Policy Dialogue, Pensions and Social Insurance Section, Discussion Paper No. IPD-01-05, October 2004).

ABOUT THE AUTHOR

Andrew G. Biggs is a resident scholar at the American Enterprise Institute (AEI), where he focuses on Social Security reform, public-sector pension financing, and analysis of compensation for public-sector employees. Prior to joining AEI, he was the principal deputy commissioner of the Social Security Administration, where he oversaw the agency's policy research efforts and led its participation in the Social Security Trustees working group. He also worked on Social Security reform at the White House National Economic Council in 2005 and was on the staff of the President's Commission to Strengthen Social Security in 2001. Mr. Biggs has an MPhil in social and political theory from Cambridge University, an MSc in financial economics from the University of London, and a PhD in government from the London School of Economics.

Printed in the USA
CPSIA information can be obtained
at www.ICGtesting.com
JSHW012045140824
68134JS00034B/3256